STICKER ENCYCLOPEDIA

Baby Animals

LONDON, NEW YORK, MELBOURNE,
MUNICH, AND DELHI

India Editorial Suchismita Banerjee,
Archana Ramachandran, Neha Pande,
Nidhilekha Mathur
India Design Romi Chakraborty,
Balwant Singh, Govind Mittal, Prashant Kumar
India DTP Sunil Sharma,
Manish Chandra Upreti, Dheeraj Arora

Consultant David Burnie
Editorial Marie Greenwood
Design Polly Appleton
US Editor Jennifer Quasha
Picture Research Rose Horridge,
Rob Nunn, Emma Shepherd
Production Editor Marc Staples
Production Rita Sinha

Design Development Manager Helen Senior
Publishing Manager Bridget Giles
Category Publisher Sue Leonard

First American Edition, 2011
Published in the United States by
DK Publishing
375 Hudson Street
New York, New York 10014

11 12 13 14 15 10 9 8 7 6 5 4 3 2 1
001—179447—July/2011

Published in Great Britain by Dorling Kindersley Limited.

A catalog record for this book is available from the Library of Congress.

ISBN 978-0-7566-8224-8

DK books are available at special discounts when purchased in bulk for sales
promotions, premiums, fund-raising, or educational use. For details,
contact: DK Publishing Special Markets, 375 Hudson Street, New York,
New York 10014 or SpecialSales@dk.com.

Printed and bound in China by L-Rex

Discover more at www.dk.com

About this book

How to use this book

You can find the stickers for each of the main information pages at the back of the book. Use the sticker outlines and labels to help you.

There are lots of extra stickers that you can use to decorate the scenes at the back of the book. It's up to you where you put them all. The most important thing is to have lots of sticker fun!

What's inside

This book is a fantastic introduction to the amazing world of baby animals. Not only will you have fun finding the right baby animal stickers, but you will learn lots of interesting facts, too.

Picture Credits

The publisher would like to thank the following for their
kind permission to reproduce their photographs:

(Key: a-above; b-below/bottom; c-centre; f-far; l-left; r-right; t-top)

Alamy Images: Arco Images GmbH / TUNS 31cr, 48clb; blickwinkel /
Kaufung 6tr; Paul Fleet 44cra; Frans Lanting Studio 31tr; Tim Gainey 33cr;
GraficallyMinded 11cra; Jonathan Hewitt 18tr; Juniors Bildarchiv / F259 49tr;
Leo Keeler 14c; Chris Mattison 49cr; Melba Photo Agency 1cl, 53tc;
MiscellaneouStock 52clb; Gerry Pearce 28bc; Wolfgang Pölzer 51cb; Anestis
Rekkas 64 (needlefish sticker); Steve Round 33bl; tbkmedia.de 15tl;
Tierfotoagentur / R. Richter 18cb; Ann and Steve Toon 9br; Duncan Usher
32crb; Lindsay Hebberd 35crb; Jared Hobbs / All Canada Photos 37br;
Hoberman Collection 8c; Carol Hughes / Gallo Images 33tl; Herbert Kehrer
53cla; Frans Lanting 20bl, 25r, 29c; Robert Lindholm / Visuals Unlimited 21cr;
Frank Lukasseck 21tl; Wayne Lynch / All Canada Photos 36cl; Thomas Marent
/ Visuals Unlimited 29crb; Charles Melton / Visuals Unlimited 34cl; Jack
Milchanowski / Visuals Unlimited 17cra; Thorsten Milse / Robert Harding
World Imagery 26cra; Momatiuk - Eastcott 37tr; Arthur Morris 42cr; David A.

Northcott 60-61 (snake sticker); Roberta Olenick / All Canada Photos 35clb;
Papilio 43cra; Lynda Richardson 27cra; Jeffrey L. Rotman 8br; Andy Rouse
41cra; Paul Souders 13c, 36bl; Lynn Stone / AgStock Images 44br; Julian
Stratenschulte / DPA 16cl; Visuals Unlimited 51cl, 53cb; Stuart Westmorland /
Science Faction 43cla; Stuart Westmorland 53bl, 64; Douglas P. Wilson / Frank
Lane Picture Agency 38tr; Tim Zurowski / All Canada Photos 29cra. **Dorling
Kindersley:** Berlin Zoo 54-55 (antelope sticker); Booth Museum of Natural
History, Brighton 45tr; Natural History Museum, London 34cr; David Peart
38-39; George Reszeter 22tr; Weymouth Sea Life Centre 51cr; Whipsnade Zoo,
Bedfordshire 41br; Jerry Young 21cl. **Dreamstime.com:** Dvin 62-63 (quail chick
sticker); Natali Goryachaya 62-63 (turkey chick sticker); Helen E. Grose 35c;
Eric Isselée 30ca, 30crb; Achmat Jappie 6-7; Marina Maslennikova 47tl;
Vladimir Melnik 30cl; Nomadimages 46c; Sallydexter 46clb. **FLPA:** Arthur
Christiansen 28cra; Flip De Nooyer / FN / Minden 47cla; Gerry Ellis / Minden
Pictures 45ca; Sumio Harada / Minden Pictures 14crb; Mitsuaki Iwago /
Minden Pictures 4-5, 22b; Colin Monteath / Minden Pictures 34bc; Flip
Nicklin / Minden Pictures 22cla; Joke Stuurman-Huitema / FN / Minden 15tr;
Norbert Wu / Minden Pictures 50c; ZSSD / Minden Pictures 15br. **Fotolia:**
Tom Curtis 37tl; Steve Lovegrove 29tl. **Getty Images:** AFP Photo DDP /
Michael Urban 47tr; AFP Photo DDP / Oliver Lang 31cl; Altrendo Nature
56-57 (coyote sticker); Anita Bugge / WireImage 45bl; Simon Dawson /
Bloomberg 18cl; De Agostini Picture Library 52c; Michael DeYoung 45cl;
Digital Vision / Digital Zoo 9ca, 16bl; Fuse 1cr, 50cr; Gallo Images / Heinrich
van den Berg 9tr; Gallo Images / Martin Harvey 4cl; Gallo Images / Travel Ink
19bl; Iconica / Jamie Grill 17clb; The Image Bank / Daisy Gilardini 42-43; The
Image Bank / Darrell Gulin 10br; The Image Bank / Doug Allan 11crb; The
Image Bank / Peter Lilja 10tr; The Image Bank / Thomas Kokta 3tr, 36tr; The
Image Bank / Winfried Wisniewski 12cl; Bruno Morandi / The Image Bank
24cl; National Geographic / Joel Sartore 56-57 (snake sticker); Pal
Teravagimov Photography / Flickr 31bc; Panoramic Images 25bl; Joe

Petersburger / National Geographic 15bl; Photodisc / Jayme Thornton 38crb;
Photographer's Choice / Burazin 16cra; Photographer's Choice / Deborah
Harrison 62-63 (elk sticker); Photographer's Choice / Frank Lukasseck 12tr;
Photographer's Choice / Martin Ruegner 10c; Photographer's Choice / Paul
Oomen 24bc; Photographer's Choice / Travelpix Ltd 25tl; Photonica / Theo
Allofs 36crb; Radius Images / Jose Luis Stephens 56-57; Riser / Manoj Shah
44clb; Riser / Stephen Frink 51bl; Joel Sartore / National Geographic 47br,
52bc; Science Faction / Stefan Sollfors 20tr; Stockbyte / Altrendo Nature 18bc;
Stone / John W Banagan 20br; Stone / Ken Graham 37bl; Jami Tarris /
Workbook Stock 11tr; Taxi / Steven W. Jones 32c; Taxi / VCL 13tc; Visuals
Unlimited / Beth Davidow 12clb; Visuals Unlimited, Inc. / Adam Jones 54-55;
Workbook Stock / Raimund Linke 19tr; Norbert Wu / Science Faction Jewels
50tr. **naturepl.com:** Andrew Harrington 27bl; Mike Wilkes 11c. **NHPA /
Photoshot:** David Higgs 46cra. **Photolibrary:** 58-59 (mink sticker);
Bildagentur RM / Tips Italia 40cr; Berndt Fischer 26cl; E. A. Janes / Age
Fotostock 3bl, 13cla; James Gerholdt / Peter Arnold Images 49cra; Guida
Gregory / Bios 47clb; Mike Hargreaves / Fresh Food Images 38clb; HSchweiger
HSchweiger 37c; Pierre Huguet / Bios 48-49; J-L. Klein & M-L. Hubert 39clb;
Frans Lemmens / Lineair 28cl; Morales Morales / Age Fotostock 8tr; Rolf
Nussbaumer / Imagebroker.net 33tc; Oxford Scientific (OSF) / Daniel J. Cox
23clb; Oxford Scientific (OSF) / Werner Bollmann 14cra; Peter Pinnock 10bl.
Science Photo Library: Douglas Faulkner 15c.

Jacket images: Front: Dorling Kindersley: Barrie Watts crb. **Back: Alamy
Images:** David Tipling cla. **Getty Images:** Stone / Tim Flach tc.

All other images © Dorling Kindersley
For further information see: **www.dkimages.com**

Contents

Looking at baby animals

Many baby animals are cute and cuddly. Some hatch out of eggs, while others are born live. Some young animals, such as baby grasshoppers, look like their parents from birth. Others, such as frogs, begin to look like their parents as they grow up.

Piglets

Piglets have four pointed toes on each foot. They use only two of these toes for walking. This means they stand on their toes like ballet dancers do.

Wolf pup

Baby wolves are called pups. When it is born, a wolf pup cannot see or hear. It is covered with short, grayish-brown fur.

DID YOU KNOW!

Piglets cannot raise their heads to look up. They can only see the sky if they lie down.

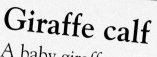

Swan

Baby swans, or cygnets, start swimming soon after birth. They swim close to their mother to stay warm and protected.

Giraffe calf

A baby giraffe, or calf, has small horns on its head and brown spots on its body. These spots help it remain hidden in the grass.

Lamb

Baby sheep are called lambs. Most lambs can stand an hour after they are born.

FACT!

A baby cobra can bite its prey the day it hatches.

Newborn

Just like your baby brother or sister, animal babies are small and helpless. They need to be fed, cleaned, and cared for. But some newborn animals, such as snakes and tortoises, can care for themselves from birth.

Calf

A calf can stand up on its wobbly legs soon after it is born, and begins to walk the same day. The calf knows its mother by her smell.

Kitten

A newborn kitten can open its eyes about a week after its birth. It cuddles close to its mother for the first three weeks of its life to keep itself warm.

FACT!

All kittens are born with blue eyes, which begin to change color after about a month.

An ostrich's egg is the largest of all birds' eggs.

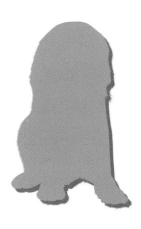

Puppy

Newborn puppies sleep a lot. For about ten days after birth, they do nothing except sleep and eat.

Chick

A chick can breathe even
when it is still inside the egg.
When a mother hen clucks,
it chirps back to her from inside.

Tiger cub

A tiger cub is born with a thick fur
coat. At first, it feeds only on its
mother's milk. The cub hunts with
its mother after about six months.

DID YOU KNOW?

A newborn ferret
is so small that
it can fit on
a teaspoon.

Tortoise

A baby tortoise breaks out of
its shell using a special egg
tooth, which falls off shortly
after hatching.

Baby mice

Newborn mice are
bald, with no fur on
their bodies. After a
couple of days, they
are covered in
soft baby fuzz.

Learning to move

Many baby animals cannot move on their own at first. Some climb on to their parents' backs. Others, such as tadpoles, begin to move around a few days after they are born.

Baby sloth

At first, the baby sloth snuggles tightly against its mother's furry belly with its claws. Later, it learns to hang upside down from trees.

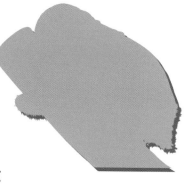

Chimpanzee

A baby chimp rides on his mother's back until he is about four years old. He clings to the fur on her neck so that he doesn't fall off.

FACT!
A baby hippopotamus is born underwater. It can swim even before it learns to walk.

Foal

About an hour after it is born, a baby horse, or foal, can walk—even trot—on its thin legs. Soon it can run by the side of its mother, but, it rests a lot, too.

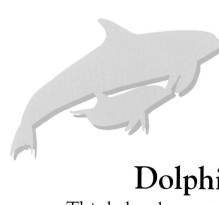

Dolphin

This baby always stays close to its mother. It swims along with her, sometimes clinging to her fin. Its mother teaches it how to dive.

Baby bird

A baby bird can fly only after its feathers have grown fully. Its parents often hold food a little away from the nest to make the baby try to fly.

Zebra foal

Soon after it is born, this foal takes baby steps on its wobbly legs. If it falls, the mother gently prods it to try again.

Ducklings

Ducklings hatch in a nest near the water's edge. After a few days, they follow their mother to the water in a single file.

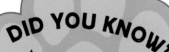

DID YOU KNOW!

A young octopus can "walk" with its eight arms on the seabed.

Baby squirrels can stand on their back legs to look around for food.

Giraffe foal

Giraffes walk in a different way from other animals. A baby giraffe first moves both feet on one side of its body. Then it moves both feet on the other side.

Family life

Many baby animals live with their families. Some babies, such as walrus calves, stay with their parents until they are nearly five years old. Others, such as baby rat snakes, take care of themselves soon after birth.

Owl family

A male owl gathers food while the female stays in the nest with her eggs. After the eggs hatch and the owlets are older, the mother helps the father hunt for food.

Penguin with chicks

Adult penguins feed and take care of their chicks. Sometimes they leave them with a group of other chicks while they go hunting for food.

FACT!

Adult panthers live in families only while they are raising their kittens.

Young angelfish swim together in shoals for protection.

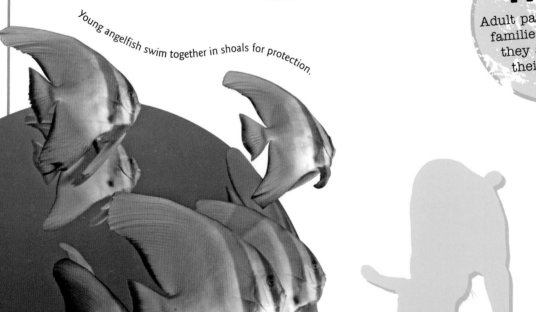

Lioness with cub

A family of lions, lionesses, and cubs is called a pride. The mothers in a pride may care for cubs that are not their own.

Elephant family

Elephants travel together in a line, each holding the tail of the one in front. If there is any sign of danger, the older elephants surround the babies to protect them.

Hyena with cubs

A hyena gives birth to its cubs in a hole in the ground. This protects them from other animals. The cubs start living on their own at the age of two.

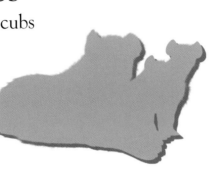

Wasp

A mother wasp builds a nest out of dried mud for her babies. She lays her eggs inside it, and then seals it so her babies are safe inside.

DID YOU KNOW?
Some badger cubs stay with their families in a sett—a generations-old maze of burrows.

Walrus and calf

If a mother walrus thinks her calf is in danger, she picks it up with her flippers, holds it close, and dives into the water.

Guinea pigs

Guinea pig pups go to their mother only when they need milk or want to be cuddled. They chirp loudly when they are hungry.

Animal litters

A group of babies born at the same time is called a litter. Some animals, such as snakes and whales, give birth to only one baby at a time. Others, such as dogs and lions, give birth to more than one.

Giant panda cubs

A giant panda gives birth to one to two cubs. The cubs start to move at three months, and live with their mother for almost three years before moving out on their own.

Cheetah cubs

A cheetah gives birth to three to five cubs at a time. Female cubs leave the group after about two years, but young males stay together for life.

FACT!
Dalmatian puppies are pure white when born. Their spots appear when they are about two weeks old.

Golden retriever pups are gentle and very friendly.

Badger cubs

Badger cubs are born in litters of two to five. They stay together until they are about 15 weeks old. After that they search for food on their own.

Hen's eggs

A hen usually lays one egg a day. After she has laid about 12 eggs, she sits on them to keep them warm. The chicks usually hatch after three weeks.

Kittens

There are two to five kittens in a litter. Kittens not only play with each other, but also with any other small animals near them.

Rabbit kits

Baby rabbits are called kits. A litter may have up to 12 kits. The mother feeds the kits for only a few minutes every day.

Meerkat pups

Meerkats can give birth to four pups at a time. When the pups are ready to come out from the burrow, the whole family stands around to watch.

DID YOU KNOW?

A kitten sleeps for about 12 hours a day.

Lambs

Sheep give birth once a year. A litter may have up to two lambs. A lamb can recognize its mother by her bleat.

Feeding

Baby animals need to eat regularly so that they stay healthy and grow faster. Some babies eat all the time, while others feed only once or twice a day. Parents feed their young in different ways.

Otter pup

Otters feed their babies milk, and later little fish, worms, and squid. After a month, the mother teaches the pups how to swim and find food on their own.

Seal pup

This pup drinks its mother's rich milk and grows very fast. When it is just one month old, it begins to swim and find food on its own.

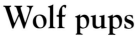

Wolf pups

A mother wolf feeds her pups with her watery milk—this keeps them from getting sick. They begin eating meat when they are 4–5 weeks old.

Goat kid

Baby goats begin to nibble on hay and green grass when they are very young. They have eight small teeth in their lower jaw for tearing the food.

Polar bear

At birth, a polar bear cub is born with no teeth, and feeds on its mother's milk. Once its mother teaches her cub to hunt, it begins to feed on its own.

DID YOU KNOW?

Guinea pig pups can eat solid food the day they are born.

Caterpillar

Caterpillars are hungry all the time. Most of them eat leaves. A few also eat the eggs of other insects, plus aphids, scale insects, and ant larvae.

Sea cow pups

Baby sea cows suckle on their mother's milk for almost a year after birth. Rich in fat, the milk helps them grow quickly and stay warm.

Baby monkey

A monkey feeds its baby just like humans do. It teaches its young how to climb trees and search for food.

A flamingo feeds milk made in its throat lining to its chick.

Playing

Just like you, baby animals love to play. Some young ones like to "play fight" with their brothers and sisters. Others, such as puppies, love to play with toys. Some baby animals may even play with you!

Baby hamster

Hamster pups like to run and need a lot of exercise. Pet hamsters enjoy running on an exercise wheel.

Tiger cubs

Tiger cubs are very playful. They love to chase each other, wrestle with their paws, and play with their mother's tail.

FACT!
Baby dolphins play by doing somersaults in the air. They love to play catch in the sea.

A baby chimp plays by making up games on its own.

Squirrel

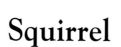

Young squirrels often scurry around and sniff everything near them. They like to chase each other up and down trees.

Fox cubs

Fox cubs love to play and fight with each other. When they are in a playful mood, they perk up their ears and rise up on their back legs.

Baby seal

Baby seals are very noisy when they play with each other. They are very smart and often start swimming just a few hours after birth.

Bear cub

A bear cub stands on its two legs when wrestling with other cubs. While playing, bear cubs may even bite each other gently.

DID YOU KNOW!

Bear cubs make a lot of noise while fighting, but they play very quietly.

Puppy

Puppies love to run free in open spaces. If you throw a ball, they will run and fetch it for you.

Baby deer

Baby deer, or fawns, are fast runners. They like to race and play tag with each other. They enjoy jumping around on their thin legs.

Keeping clean

Like you, baby animals need to bathe and keep clean. Some baby animals clean themselves using their tongues, beaks, or paws. Other young are kept clean by their parents.

Baby elephant

Baby elephants love to play in water. They fill their trunks with water and spray it all over themselves.

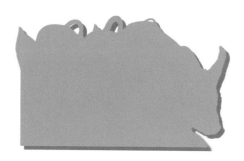

Piglets

Piglets are not as dirty as many people think. They have different places in their pens for eating, sleeping, and pooping.

Rabbit kit

This rabbit kit looks neat and clean because its mother licks it everyday.

FACT!
After rain, a hummingbird licks water droplets off its chick to keep it dry.

Bobcat kitten

Like all kittens, baby bobcats love to be squeaky clean. They spend a lot of time licking their bodies to clean themselves.

Baby baboon

This baby baboon is kept clean by its mother. She parts its hair and picks fleas and ticks off its body.

Swan cygnets

Cygnets use their beaks to clean themselves. They can turn their necks around completely to clean the feathers on their wings and backs.

Baby ant

Baby ants are licked clean by a nurse ant, one of the worker ants in an ant colony.

DID YOU KNOW?

Baby birds use their beaks to clean their feathers. This is known as preening.

A cow licks its newborn calf clean.

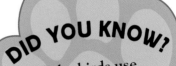

Baby gecko

A baby gecko does not need to keep clean since it sheds its skin so often. It turns pale just before its skin begins to peel off.

Carrying babies

Not all baby animals can walk or move on their own. Their parents carry them on their backs or in pouches. Some animals, such as wombats, carry their babies in their pouches. Others, such as crocodiles, carry their young ones in their mouths.

Wolf spider

After they hatch from their eggs, baby wolf spiders quickly climb up their mother's legs. They ride on her back till they grow up.

A young lemur rides on its mother's back for protection.

FACT!

A male midwife toad carries the eggs wrapped around on his back legs.

Sea horse

A male sea horse takes care of the eggs laid by the mother. The father keeps the eggs safe in a pouch until they hatch.

Kangaroo

A baby kangaroo, or joey, lives in its mother's pouch for three months after birth. Then it climbs out to move around on its own, but returns to the pouch to feed and sleep.

Poison dart frog

After the eggs hatch, the mother frog carries her tadpoles on her back, and places them in water pools on big leaves. The tadpoles stay there until they grow up.

Opossum

The mother opossum carries her young in a pouch. Later the babies ride on her back. Sometimes, they hold onto her tail so they don't fall off.

Cougar

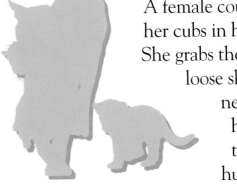

A female cougar carries her cubs in her mouth. She grabs them by the loose skin on their necks so that her sharp teeth do not hurt them.

Scorpion

Baby scorpions travel on their mother's back until they are old enough to move around by themselves.

Orangutan

A young orangutan clings on to its mother's stomach until it is about a year old. It also rides on her back as she swings from one branch to another.

DID YOU KNOW?
A male jawfish carries the eggs in his mouth until they hatch. He does not eat during this time.

Sleeping

Baby animals sleep a lot. Many of them wake up only to feed or play. Some baby animals cling to their mothers while sleeping. Others sleep alone, or cuddle up with the other babies to take naps.

Swift chick

A baby swift sleeps for long hours in its nest. Later, when it starts to fly, it sleeps in the air while flying.

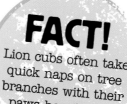

Dolphin calf

A dolphin calf sleeps very little for about one month after its birth. It follows its mother as she swims.

FACT!

Lion cubs often take quick naps on tree branches with their paws hanging on either side.

Ball python snakelet

A baby ball python coils up into a ball and sleeps with its eyes open. Its spotted skin helps it hide among trees.

A lion cub sleeps close to its mother.

Bat pup

This young bat sleeps hanging upside down from its hooked claws. It wraps its wings around its body, like a jacket, while sleeping.

Baby angelfish

Baby fish don't have eyelids, so they sleep with their eyes open. Many baby fish burrow into the mud of the sea floor to sleep.

Baby horse

A baby horse, or foal, sleeps lying on its side, sometimes with its legs folded in. When it grows older, it sleeps standing up, like its parents.

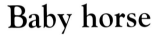

Baby koala

A baby koala, or joey, sleeps inside a pouch on its mother's belly for the first six months. Later, it climbs up to its mother's back and sleeps, hugging her.

DID YOU KNOW?

A baby giraffe sleeps standing up with one eye open all the time.

Kittens

Newborn kittens sleep most of the time. They curl up close together in groups and fall fast asleep.

Baby animal homes

Animals build nests, burrows, or dens to raise their young. Some make their homes in very cold places covered with snow. Others live in hot, sandy deserts. Oceans, rivers, and lakes are also home to many animals. Here are some of the different types of places where animals live.

Riverbanks

A riverbank is the muddy land at the side of a river. Animals found here, such as turtles, crocodiles, and water birds, can live both on land and in water.

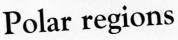

Deserts

Deserts are dry places with little water, so few plants grow here. Deserts are usually covered with sand or rocks. They can be hot or cold.

Polar regions

The northernmost (Arctic) and the southernmost (Antarctic) regions are the coldest places on Earth. The sea is mostly covered with ice.

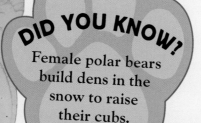

DID YOU KNOW?
Female polar bears build dens in the snow to raise their cubs.

Forests

Forests are large areas where lots of trees and plants grow. Tree animals, such as squirrels, and burrowing animals, such as moles, live here.

FACT!

A cuckoo does not build its own nest. It lays its eggs in the nests of other birds.

Grasslands

Grass, shrubs, and bushes grow in grasslands. They are home to grass-eating animals, such as zebras and antelope, and meat eaters, such as lions and cheetahs.

Grasslands

Grasslands are huge areas filled with grasses and varieties of trees and shrubs. They are home to herds of grazing animals, such as zebra and bison. Baby animals sometimes hide in the long grass while their parents go out searching for food.

FACT!
Fawns give out very little scent. This protects them from bigger animals in the grasslands.

Vulture chick

Young vultures start flying when they are 10–11 weeks old. Chicks use their sharp eyesight to hunt for dead animals in the grasslands.

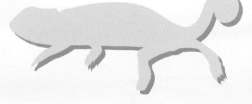

Baby chameleon

All chameleon babies can change color from birth. This baby has changed its color to green to hide among the leaves and catch insects.

Ostrich chick

These chicks hide under their parents' wings to find shelter from the sun and rain. Sometimes, they lie flat in the dry grass. This way bigger animals can't see them.

Lion cub

A lioness hides her newborn cubs in thick bushes for about six weeks. Later she teaches her young how to sneak up on their prey and catch them.

Fawn

This young fawn's coat is reddish brown with white spots on its back. This helps it hide easily among the trees and escape from any animals that may hunt it.

DID YOU KNOW!

A baby zebra can start eating grass 15 days after it is born.

Baby tortoise

Baby tortoises are land animals. They feed on grass, leaves, and flowers. Some also eat worms or insect larvae.

Ferret kit

These kits are born in dens left by prairie dogs in the grasslands. Mothers hunt small animals, such as rabbits or lizards, and bring the meat for the kits to the den.

Jackal pups

These pups are born in thick bushes or holes. The mother jackal changes her home every two weeks to protect the pups.

Deserts

Deserts are hot, dry places with miles of sand and little water. Some young animals, such as gerbils, have a furry bottom to protect them from the heat of the sand. Others, such as baby camels, drink a lot of water all at once, so they don't need water for months.

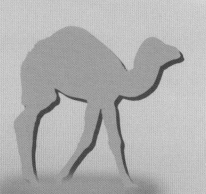

FACT!
A baby camel opens and closes its nose to keep out sand and dust.

Baby jerboa
This baby jerboa has very long legs. It uses them to jump quickly and hop huge distances across the desert.

Baby camel
A newborn camel does not have a hump. When the baby starts eating solid food, the hump begins to grow.

Dingo pup
Dingo pups eat desert animals such as lizards and rats. The pups' parents hunt these animals for them.

Baby lizard
As soon as they hatch, baby lizards hide under stones. They do this to protect themselves from the hot desert sun.

Baby thorny devil

This baby lizard has spines all over its body—even around its eyes. When it rains, water droplets run down the spines straight into its mouth.

Desert scorpion

A baby desert scorpion uses its eight legs to crawl over rocky desert. It usually comes out at night, when it is cooler.

Roadrunner chick

These chicks are born in nests made on shrubs or clusters of cactus plants. Their long legs help them run around quickly to catch insects.

Sidewinder snakelet

This young snake moves by shifting its whole body sideways. This helps it move easily on the slippery desert sand.

Desert locust

This young locust, or hopper, is born without wings. It walks across sandy soil.

Rainforests

Rainforests, or jungles, are hot, lush forests that get a lot of rain. Here baby animals survive in different ways. Some hide in nests on tall trees or thick bushes. Others simply stick close to their mothers for protection.

Baby pygmy marmoset

This five-week-old pygmy marmoset can climb up trees without its parents' help. Its small size helps it hide from other jungle animals.

Toucan chicks

These young toucans use their large beaks to pick fruit from trees. As the chicks grow, so do their beaks.

FACT!

A male hornbill drops food for his chicks through a small hole in their closed nest.

Tree frog

This young tree frog, or tadpole, is brown. Its color helps it hide among the rainforest trees and escape animals that might feed on it.

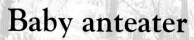

Baby anteater

A baby anteater is born with a full coat of hair and looks just like its parents. It often rides on its mother's back to hide from bigger jungle animals.

Baby macaw

Three-month-old macaws feed on
fruit and seeds found in the jungle.
They quickly learn from their parents
which fruit to pick from which tree
at different times of the year.

Baby chimpanzee

A baby chimp learns how
to walk, climb, and eat by
watching its mother.
When a little older, it
builds its own sleeping
nest on treetops.

Jaguar cub

A jaguar cub can easily go
into water and catch fish like
its parents. Jaguars live
near rivers and swamps,
or in thick rainforests.

DID YOU KNOW!

A baby stick insect
looks like a tree
twig. This helps
it hide from
forest animals.

Baby hornbill

Baby hornbills are born
in sealed nests inside
tree trunks. They break
out of the nest once
they can take care
of themselves.

Forests and woodlands

Forests and woodlands are home to many baby animals. Here they feed on leaves and fruit. The thick bushes and shrubs also offer many places to hide from larger animals.

Raccoon kit

This baby was born with its eyes closed. Its eyes opened after 20 days. It can now follow its mother in search of food.

Quail chick

Quail chicks hatch out of their eggs in less than a month. They can leave the nest with their parents soon after hatching.

FACT!
Baby raccoons spend their first two months living in holes in tall trees.

Baby hedgehog

This baby has soft spines at birth. Later harder spines grow in their place.

Baby squirrel

A newborn squirrel has no hair or teeth for up to three weeks. Once its teeth grow fully, it chews on tree branches to sharpen them.

Baby centipedes

Some baby centipedes are born with a few pairs of legs. They keep growing more pairs as they grow older.

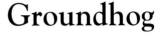

Groundhog

Baby groundhogs are born in burrows under the ground. They come out six to seven weeks after birth.

Baby mole

A baby mole has very sharp claws. When it is older it grows thick fur all over its body, except on its pink paws and nose.

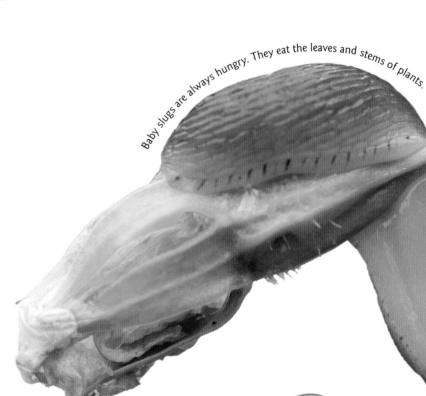

Baby slugs are always hungry. They eat the leaves and stems of plants.

Blue tit chick

Adult blue tits have blue and yellow feathers. But their chicks are duller looking, and have green and yellow feathers.

DID YOU KNOW?

Some baby slugs have a tiny shell on their backs, just near the tail.

Mountains

Life can be difficult for animals living high up in the mountains. Some baby animals grow thick fur to keep warm from the cold. Others develop strong feet to climb up cliffs. This helps them live on rocky hilltops and steep slopes, or in thick mountain forests.

FACT!
When excited, yak babies run with their tails held high over their backs.

Cave cricket

This young cricket uses its long antennae to explore caves and other dark places. It can also jump very high.

Hummingbird chick

These babies cannot fly until, at three weeks old, they grow feathers and can fly backward, sideways, and even hover in midair.

Baby llama

A baby llama's mother hums to it when it is born. All the female llamas in the herd surround it at birth to protect it from preying animals.

Baby red panda

This shy baby eats solid food three months after its birth. It eats mainly bamboo shoots found in the mountains.

Eaglet

This young eagle is born with very small toes. After about 20 weeks, its claws become strong enough to carry prey through the air.

Snow leopard cub

A snow leopard cub is born blind and helpless with a thick coat of fur. This helps it stay warm in cold, snowy mountain tops.

DID YOU KNOW!

A baby red panda wraps its ringed tail around itself to stay warm.

Mountain goat kid

A mountain goat kid can climb a few days after birth. But its mother keeps it on a rocky cliff or ledge high in the mountains for protection.

Baby yak

A baby yak has a thick, hairy coat. This protects it from the cool mountain air. At night, adult yaks huddle around the baby to keep it warm.

Polar regions

Polar regions are the icy areas of the Arctic and the Antarctic. Most baby animals living here have a thick hairy coat to protect them from the cold. Others have strong feet to walk in deep snow or white fur to hide from bigger animals in the snow.

Harp seal pup

A harp seal pup is born with white fur. This protects it from the cold. After two weeks, this fur is replaced by a gray coat.

Penguin chick

The fluffy feathers on this baby's flippers become smooth and waterproof a month after birth. It can then use its flippers to swim.

FACT!

A baby reindeer can run faster than a human.

Baby reindeer

A baby reindeer, or fawn, is born without horns. The horns grow when it is about a year old. Its thick brown fur turns gray in winter.

Arctic fox pup

A newborn Arctic fox has brown fur. This turns white as it grows older. Its thick, padded paws help it walk on slippery ice.

Albatross chick

An albatross chick feeds on the fish and squid that its parents catch. Once the chick's wings grow, it flies away from its nest to live at sea.

Arctic tern chick

These chicks are born in nests on flat ground. Once they hatch, they leave their nests and hide among stones and small plants.

Polar bear cubs stay in snow dens to keep warm.

Arctic hare

A baby Arctic hare, or leveret, can hop on its back legs like a kangaroo.

DID YOU KNOW?

A female polar bear carries her cubs on her back when there is deep snow.

Baby moose

A newborn moose has red fur. This changes to brown as it grows. Its long legs and big hooves keep it from sinking into thick snow.

Oceans

The ocean is home to different fish and other sea creatures. Many young, such as baby octopuses, hatch out of eggs laid at the bottom of the ocean. Others, such as baby blue whales, are born near the surface of the water.

Shark pup

Some sharks, such as this dogfish shark, hatch out of eggs. Others, such as bull sharks, give birth to live young.

Baby lumpfish

The green color of this baby lumpfish helps it hide among plants and escape bigger sea creatures.

FACT!

A growing crab is called a "megalops," which means big eyes.

Baby octopus

A young octopus can spray a special dark-colored ink. This colors the water around it and scares bigger animals nearby.

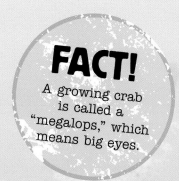

Baby jellyfish

After birth, baby jellyfish stick to a rock or shell in the water, and stay there until they grow up. Once they're older, they use their arms to sweep food into their mouths.

Baby clown triggerfish

A young clown triggerfish has white spots all over its body. As it grows up, it develops leopard-like brown spots.

Baby eel

A baby eel is born in the ocean. As it grows, it moves to rivers and lakes where it feeds on shrimp, worms, and insects.

Baby blue whale

A newborn baby whale is as heavy as an adult hippopotamus. It stays with its mother for about a year after birth.

DID YOU KNOW?

A newborn cuttlefish can eat a shrimp twice its own size the day it hatches.

Baby lobster

A baby lobster has a hard shell on its body to protect it. As it grows older, it breaks out of its old shell and grows a new one.

Rivers, lakes, swamps

Some baby animals, such as tadpoles, are born underwater. Others, such as ducklings, hatch on land, and slowly make their way to the water, often led by their parent.

Crocodile

A baby crocodile lies still in shallow water, waiting for prey. It leaps out in a flash and snaps up insects, frogs, fish, and other small animals.

Duckling

This duckling dips its beak in water to feed. It uses its beak like a strainer to scoop out small plants.

FACT!

A tadpole's tail slowly disappears as it changes into a frog.

Beaver pup

A mother beaver rubs its pup with her paws. This covers the fur with a layer of oil, which makes the coat waterproof.

River otter

If an otter pup is frightened of water, its mother gently nudges and pushes the pup toward it.

Dragonfly nymph

A dragonfly nymph has a pair of sharp jaws attached to its lower lip. These are folded back under its head. It shoots them out to catch water insects.

Tadpole

A tadpole's long tail helps it swim easily. Like a fish, a tadpole breathes using gills. It has no legs or arms.

Young kingfisher

This young bird's first dive into water happens about four days after leaving its nest. The parent drops fish into water for the young one to catch.

DID YOU KNOW?

Young crocodiles are often eaten by adult crocodiles.

Baby rhinoceros

A rhino calf enjoys hanging around in muddy swamps. On a hot day, the calf cools itself by wallowing in marshes and lakes.

Baby animal groups

All kinds of animals live on this Earth. They can be divided into five main groups. An animal may be a mammal, bird, fish, reptile or amphibian, or an invertebrate.

Mammal

A red fox is a mammal. This baby red fox has a brown or gray coat that turns red when it is about a month old. It feeds on its mother's milk.

Bird

An egret is a bird. These egret chicks have fuzzy white feathers. Egrets use their sharp bills to catch fish in water.

Amphibian

A salamander is an amphibian. This young tiger salamander is brown with dark spots that later turn to bars or irregular shapes. Many are born in water, and then move to land.

DID YOU KNOW?

Baby penguins cannot fly. They use their flippers for swimming in cold waters.

FACT!

Baby scorpions are born live. They do not hatch out of eggs.

Invertebrate

A tarantula spider is an invertebrate. This baby sheds its skin many times a year as it grows. It can grow up to be as big as a dinner plate.

Fish

A parrotfish is a kind of fish. It gets its name because its teeth form a parrot-like beak. The body of a young parrotfish changes color as it grows up.

Mammals

Most baby mammals grow fur or hair on their bodies. They breathe with their lungs and feed on their mothers' milk. Most mammals give birth to live young.

A baby squirrel monkey has a long tail.

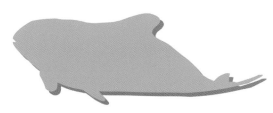

Baby whale

When a baby whale is hungry, it bumps its mother. She then squirts thick milk into its mouth.

FACT!

A baby platypus is born with webbed feet, which helps it swim.

Baby donkey

A baby donkey, or foal, has a thick, fluffy coat. Its ears are long and pointed.

Baby hippo

A baby hippo is born underwater. As soon as it is born, its mother gently pushes it to the surface to breathe.

Baby wombat

A baby wombat is carried in its mother's pouch for about five months. Once it is out of the pouch, it starts nibbling on grass.

Baby platypus

Unlike other baby mammals, this baby hatches from an egg. It has a bill like a duck. When it is older, it uses its bill to scoop out worms from water.

Skunk kit

This skunk kit, like its parents, has a coat of shiny black fur with white stripes running down its body.

DID YOU KNOW?
A baby wombat is called a joey. When born, it is the size of a jellybean.

Black panther cub

This cub has blackish brown fur. Mother and cub greet each other by rubbing their faces or bodies together.

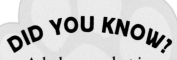

Baby mongoose

A baby mongoose is born in a burrow. It feeds on its mother's milk until it starts hunting for food on its own.

Birds

All birds have feathers and two feet. They have a beak, but no teeth. Birds lay eggs, and chicks hatch out of these eggs. Most chicks cannot see when they are born.

Baby robin

Baby robins are born with very few feathers. But after two weeks they grow full feathers and can move their wings.

Emu chick

Emu chicks are born with brown and white stripes. This makes it hard for bigger animals to find them in the grass.

FACT!
Unlike most eggs laid by birds, the shells of a robin's eggs are light blue.

Kiwi chick

A kiwi's eggs are bigger than those of a hen. A newborn chick has a lot of fuzzy hair, which sometimes makes it look larger than its parents.

Baby parrot

Newborn parrots have no feathers. Later they grow green, red, or even gray feathers.

Swallow chick

Adult swallows feed their
chicks insects rolled into
a ball. They feed the chicks
as many as 20 insects
at a time.

Baby stork

This young stork is learning
to fly. Its beak is now black
but it will start turning red
when it is three months old.

Woodpecker

This chick is fed by its
parents when young. Later
it learns how to use its sharp
beak and dig holes in trees.

DID YOU KNOW?

Peacocks do
not grow their
colorful feathers
until they are two
years old.

Peachicks learn to feed by following their mother.

Dove squab

Parent doves make a milky
substance in their throats.
A baby dove, or squab,
pokes its beak into its
parent's throat to drink it.

Reptiles and amphibians

Reptiles, such as snakes and lizards, have rough, scaly skin. Amphibians, such as salamanders and toads, have smooth, damp skin. Most baby reptiles and amphibians hatch from eggs. They live both on land and in water.

DID YOU KNOW?
Baby Komodo dragons grow up to become the largest lizards on Earth.

Toad

This young toad is born in water. It has a small tail that disappears when it grows into an adult.

Baby salamander

This young salamander sprays a poisonous liquid from its skin to protect itself.

A baby ringneck snake is born with a colored ring around its neck.

Komodo dragon

A baby Komodo dragon rolls in its own poop. The foul smell protects it from adult Komodos.

Baby alligator

A baby alligator is born on land. Its mother later carries it in her mouth and takes it to the water. Its flat tail helps it swim.

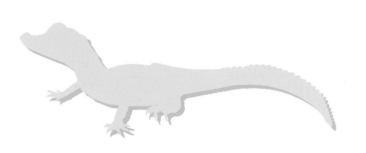

Gila monster

A young Gila monster feeds on the eggs of other reptiles. If they are buried underground, it uses its sharp claws to dig them up.

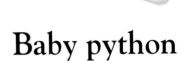

Baby python

When hunting, this young python wraps its slender body tightly around its prey.

Baby frilled lizard

This baby lizard opens up the bright orange-and-yellow frill around its neck to scare other animals.

FACT!

A baby snake sheds its outer layer of skin many times as it grows.

Baby iguana

This bright green baby iguana has sharp claws that help it climb trees. It may shed its tail if chased.

Fish

All fish live in water. Baby fish breathe through their gills and swim with the help of their fins. They have scales on their body.

Swordfish

This young swordfish is so called because of its sword-like bill. Once it grows up, it uses this bill to hunt its prey in the ocean waters.

Pygmy shark

A baby pygmy shark's belly lights up in the dark. It grows up to be only as big as a man's hand.

Koi fish

These babies can be different colors, such as silver, red, blue, or yellow. Their colored scales can take up to a year to appear.

Piranha

Piranhas are dangerous creatures that can eat their prey live. This young piranha eats the fins and flesh of other fish that come near it.

FACT!
Some sharks can give birth to nearly a hundred babies at a time.

Baby goldfish don't have a stomach to store food.

Frogfish

This young frogfish can walk on the seabed using its fins like a pair of legs. It can also "gallop" by moving its front fins together.

DID YOU KNOW?

Newborn goldfish are shiny brown in color. They turn golden when they are a year old.

Catfish

After hatching, baby catfish stay in their nests for about ten days. Later, they start looking for food on their own.

Herring

Young herrings feed on small fish. The herrings take about four years to develop fully.

Butterfly fish

This baby is born with sharp pointed bones on its body. These protect it from being eaten by larger fish. The bones disappear as it grows up.

Invertebrates

Animals that don't have a backbone are called invertebrates. This group includes all insects. Some invertebrates, such as snails, hatch out of eggs. Others, such as baby scorpions, are born live.

Jewel beetle

A baby jewel beetle, or grub, is born white and legless. As it grows, it develops a colorful metallic shine.

FACT!
Baby tarantulas eat the yolk sac from which they hatch.

Baby silkworm

Newborn silkworms are covered with tiny black hair. Later, they shed their skin and turn white in color.

Tarantula

The female tarantula spider lays her eggs in a silken bag called an egg sac. After hatching, each spiderling digs its own burrow.

DID YOU KNOW?

Some caterpillars give out a bad smell to keep away dangerous wasps and flies.

Baby starfish

A baby starfish is not star shaped like its parents. It develops this shape as it grows older. This young starfish now looks like its parents.

Baby snail

The first thing a baby snail does after birth is find food. It usually eats its own eggshell. At times, it also eats the other unhatched eggs.

Cricket

Baby crickets eat a lot of plants. Sometimes they eat even more than their parents.

Baby sea anemone

Sea anemone babies grow attached to the bottom of the adult. They break off when they are big enough to live on their own.

Baby crab

A young crab has a hard outer case covering its body. The crab replaces the case with a bigger one every time it grows.

This caterpillar will eventually turn into a beautiful butterfly.

Grassland

Checklist

Use the stickers in this book to fill the scene. Here are some animals that live in grasslands. Add others too!

- ☐ Antelope
- ☐ Zebra
- ☐ Giraffe
- ☐ Rhinoceros
- ☐ Tiger
- ☐ Ferret
- ☐ Jackal
- ☐ Elephant
- ☐ Ostrich
- ☐ Deer

Desert

Checklist

Use the stickers in the book to fill the desert scene. These are some of the baby animals you might find here:

- [ ] Rattlesnake
- [ ] Gila monster
- [ ] Thorny devil
- [ ] Jerboa
- [ ] Roadrunner
- [ ] Camel
- [ ] Lizard
- [ ] Scorpion
- [ ] Coyote
- [ ] Dingo

Riverbank

Checklist

Use the stickers in the book to fill the scene. These are some animals you will find here. Can you find any others?

- [ ] Crocodile
- [ ] Beaver
- [ ] Kingfisher
- [ ] River otter
- [ ] Dragonfly
- [ ] Mink
- [ ] Toad
- [ ] Hippopotamus
- [ ] Duck
- [ ] Salamander

Rainforest

Checklist

Use the stickers at the
back of the book to fill
this lush, green rainforest.
Here are some animals
that live here:

- Pygmy marmoset
- Green tree python
- Howler monkey
- Caterpillar
- Macaw
- Jaguar
- Anteater
- Toucan
- Tree frog
- Parrot

Mountainous forest

Checklist

Use the stickers in this book to fill the scene. Here's a list of animals to help you. How many do you recognize?

- [ ] Llama
- [ ] Hedgehog
- [ ] Raccoon
- [ ] Centipede
- [ ] Mountain quail
- [ ] Mole
- [ ] Elk
- [ ] Turkey
- [ ] Red panda
- [ ] Fox

Ocean

Checklist

Use the stickers in this book to fill the ocean scene. These are some of the animals that live here. Which is your favorite?

- [ ] Sea horse
- [ ] Blue whale
- [ ] Dolphin
- [ ] Jellyfish
- [ ] Salmon
- [ ] Lobster
- [ ] Garfish
- [ ] Octopus
- [ ] Shark
- [ ] Clown triggerfish

Penguin with chicks

Baby chameleon

Badger cubs

Hyena with cubs

Baby llama

Baby whale

Baby seal

Lion cub

Meerkat

Wasp

Baby lumpfish

Fox cubs

Giraffe with foal

Baby lobster

Squirrel

Baby rhinoceros

Piglets

River otter

Dragonfly nymph

Dove squab

Cheetah cubs

Wolf with pups

Tadpole

Tortoise

Otter pup

Kittens

Baby stork

Lambs

Baby blue whale

Baby horse

Emu chick

Baby gecko

Baby moose

Zebra foal

Baby hamster

Chimpanzee

Elephant family

Dolphin

Young kingfisher

Baby monkey

Kitten

Baby alligator

Ducklings

Baby sea
anemone

Polar bear

Kangaroo

Tiger cub

Penguin chick

Baby silkworm

Baby hippo

Baby macaw

Puppy

Goat kid

Orangutan
with baby

Jackal pups

family

Swan cygnets

Tiger cubs

Baby eel

Crocodile

Ostrich chick

Ferret kit

deer

Hen with eggs

Bear cub

Lioness with cub

Rabbit kits

Foal

Vulture chick

Giant panda cubs

Caterpillar

Baby tortoise

Calf

Baby clown triggerfish

Baboon with baby

Cougar with cubs

Baby ant

Baby iguana

Baby elephant

Shark pup

Bobcat kitten

Arctic fox pup

Toucan chicks

Desert scorpion

Piranha

Rabbit kit

Poison dart frog

Gila monster

Baby reindeer

Baby hornbill

Scorpion

Opossum

Harp seal pup

Swift chick

Ball python
snakelet

Baby mice

Kiwi chick

Puppy

Baby squirrel

Quail chick

Eaglet

Snow leopard cub

Catfish

Swordfish

Baby crab

Seal pup

Baby anteater

Bat pup

Baby
red panda

Desert locust

Pygmy
shark

Baby donkey

Mountain
goat kid

Beaver pup

Baby octopus

Skunk kit

Baby jerboa

Hummingbird chick

Dolphin calf

Komodo dragon

Woodpecker

ar cub

Baby wombat

Blue tit chick

Tarantula

Baby pygmy marmoset

Baby jellyfish

Dingo pup

Baby hedgehog

Jewel beetle

Roadrunner chick

Baby thorny devil

Arctic hare

Herring

Arctic tern chick

Fawn

Duckling

Baby mongoose

Baby yak

Guinea pigs

Baby platypus

starfish

Cave cricket

Sidewinder
snakelet

Baby koala

Baby lizard

Baby bird

Albatross chick

Baby sloth

Tree frog

Sea cow pups

Baby chimpanzee

Raccoon kit

Baby camel

Koi fish

Baby mole

Toad

Baby salamand

Frogfish

Swallow chick

Baby python

Baby rob

Walrus and calf

Kittens

Baby angelfish

Wolf spider

Chick

Butterfly fish

Sea horse

Cricket

Baby snail

Baby parrot

Black panther cub

Baby centipedes

Groundhog

Baby frilled li